To Joanne
from ♡
Marion and Bill
Christmas, 1962

Vincent van Gogh

GREAT ART OF THE AGES

———————

Vincent

GREAT ART OF THE AGES

van Gogh

Text by MEYER SCHAPIRO

Department of Art History and Archaeology, Columbia University

Harry N. Abrams, Inc. Publishers, New York

Milton S. Fox, EDITOR

STUDY OF A TREE
Crayon heightened with white
April 1882
Kröller-Müller State Museum
Otterlo, Holland

Vincent van Gogh

(1853-1890)

WHAT MAKES VAN GOGH A UNIQUE ARTIST is his power of giving us at the same time a most vivid sense of the qualities of things and an equally compelling revelation of his own feelings. In his painting of a sunflower or peasant or wheatfield, we enjoy the beauty and vitality of simple objects; but he communicates also his overflowing passionateness, his ecstatic appreciation and something of the loneliness and need for love which had brought him to art as a means of reaching others. He achieves this high expressiveness by a daring use of color, more intense than in previous art, with new and surprising harmonies; and also by the vigor of his brush-strokes and lines. In all the elements of his art we experience the force of his conviction and his exaltation before things. In realistic painting, artists are more often subdued by the task of minute observation, and in romantic

5

art we are taken far from the everyday world into a rarefied and artificial atmosphere. In van Gogh the opposites of reality and emotion are united and reconciled. The familiar objects he paints belong both to nature and to loving, desiring, suffering man. His art has helped to educate our eyes and to unloosen our feelings. It is an art that springs not from ideas — although van Gogh was a thoughtful mind — but from a great faith in humanity and an urgent, irrepressible need for communication. That faith and need mark his whole life-story — a tragic struggle ending in madness and suicide.

Vincent van Gogh was born in 1853 at Groot Zundert, the son of a country parson. As a boy he was shy, fond of books and pictures, a solitary rambler in the woods and fields. At sixteen, through an uncle, he went to The Hague to work in a picture gallery, and for the next seven years was employed in branches of the same firm in Brussels, London and Paris. During this time he got to know painting intimately. Rembrandt and Millet were his great loves, but he admired also the sentimental artists who pictured the sufferings of the poor and abandoned. In London, he began to doubt himself and his job; a rebuff from a girl he loved was the starting point of his despair. Intensely religious, he became a lay preacher, and after some years prepared for the ministry. Failing to meet the requirements—theology and Greek were too much for his passionate nature, eager for a direct communion with souls—he turned to missionary work among the Belgian miners. He wished to share their poverty and to comfort them, but his radical Christian zeal scandalized his church. Drawing this wretched world and finding some consolation in his clumsy efforts to represent what he saw and felt, he resolved at twenty-seven, after a period of wandering and depressing uncertainty, to

STUDIES OF HANDS
Black crayon. January 1885
Stedelijk Museum, Amsterdam
(V. W. van Gogh Collection)

6

OPPOSITE PAGE:
SIDEWALK CAFE AT NIGHT
Commentary on page 39

become a painter; art, he thought, was his only means of salvation, a solitary and pure activity, in which he would be free, responsible to himself alone, and yet might create a work that would give joy and understanding to others. It would also unite him with the great masters, men who for Vincent had the spiritual quality of saints and martyrs. For a short while, he studied with Mauve, a respected painter of landscape; but for the most part he learned by himself, drawing, painting, reading, studying the pictures of others, with a fanatical earnestness. During this period of preparation between 1880 and 1885, he provoked hostility and misunderstanding; he was frustrated in a passionate love by the woman's family; his own parents stood in the way of his marriage with another woman; and a drunken prostitute whom he nursed in compassion and with whom he lived for a while, supporting also her two illegitimate children, disappointed him. By this time he had lost his Christian faith. His one sure support was his younger brother, Theo, an employee in a gallery in Paris and a loyal friend of the still unpopular Impressionists and their disciples. Without Theo's generous help, Vincent could scarcely have managed to paint. His letters to Theo are a monument to the two brothers, a testimony of a great friendship as well as a masterpiece of self-revelation. In 1885, after four years of intense study in Holland, Vincent left for Antwerp, and some months later, in 1886, came to Paris. Here he discovered a new art, of a luminosity and a richness of color he had not known before; under the influence of the Impressionists and of Japanese prints, his palette lightened, his stroke became freer, and his subject matter more joyous. He met Toulouse-Lautrec, Gauguin, Seurat, Pissarro and Cézanne during his two years in Paris. But unhappy in the metropolis, sick, hungry, and ill at ease among people, with whom he often quarreled, he left for Arles in February 1888, hoping to find in the south of France a more healthful climate and a world of color congenial to the new aims of his art. He returned to the peasant and landscape subjects of his Holland days, but now they were themes of vitality and love and joy in living, completely free of the somberness of his first pictures. He dreamed of creating in Arles a colony of painters who would work together, sharing a common life. Gauguin joined him in October. There on Christmas Eve, after weeks of strain, van Gogh suffered a mental crisis; he attacked his friend and cut off his own ear. Recovering, he was able to paint pictures with little or no trace of his disturbed condition. But after recurring crises, in deep melancholy, he moved to an asylum at St. Rémy, near Arles. His work now entered a new phase, of a brooding, tragic expression, with subdued colors and intricately coiling lines, yet no less masterly than the paintings of Arles. In May 1890 he put himself under the care of a Dr. Gachet in Auvers, a village near Paris. By this time Vincent was becoming known as an artist; he was invited to exhibit in an important show in Brussels, where Cézanne, Renoir and Seurat had also exhibited; and in the first number of the *Mercure de France*, in January 1890, appeared a warm appreciation of his art and personality. His painting in Auvers is sometimes joyous, sometimes filled with anxiety. In despair over his persisting depression and the prospect of further struggles (he feared also to be a burden to Theo who had married and was not doing well financially), he shot himself on July 27, 1890. Theo died not long after and was buried beside him in the cemetery of Auvers.

STARRY SKY AND CYPRESSES
Pen and ink. Autumn 1889
Kunsthalle, Bremen

PAINTED APRIL-MAY 1885, NEUNEN

The Potato Eaters

OIL ON CANVAS, 32¼ x 44⅞″

STEDELIJK MUSEUM, AMSTERDAM *(V. W. van Gogh Collection)*

CONCEIVED AS A SUMMATION OF VAN GOGH'S WORK and study up to that time, it also expresses most strongly and fully his social and moral feelings. He was a painter of peasants, not for the sake of their picturesqueness—although he was moved by their whole aspect—but from a deep affinity and solidarity with poor people, whose lives, like his own, were burdened with care. He found in their common meal the occasion in which their humanity and moral beauty are strikingly revealed; they appear then as a close community, based upon work and the sharing of the fruits of work. The table is their altar and the food a sacrament for each one who has labored. Under the single light at this common table, the solitude of the individual is overcome and the harshness of nature, too; yet each figure retains a thought of its own and two of them seem to be on the brink of an unspoken loneliness. The colors of the dark interior, blue, green and brown, bring us back to nature outside. In the homely faces and hands of these peasants—in color and modeling they are like the potatoes that nourish them—there is a touching purity. It is the purity of familial souls in whom care for one another and the hard struggle with the earth and weather leave little place for self-striving.

The composition has a rough strength, in part the result of a naïve placing. And in van Gogh's clumsiness, which conveys also, as he intended, the clumsiness of his people, there is a source of movement. The grouping of the figures at the sides of the table is odd; the wall between the two figures at the right creates a strange partitioning of the intimate space.

Within the gloom of the dark tonality are remarkable bits of painting, prepared by his tenacious studies: the cups of coffee, with their grey shadows; the potatoes on the platter; and the superb heads which, in their isolation from one another, betray the portrait studies from which they were copied. The eyes of the two figures at the left shine with an inner light and the shadows on their features are more a modeling of character than a phenomenon of darkness. "I like so much better to paint the eyes of people than to paint cathedrals," van Gogh wrote shortly after.

10

PAINTED 1887, PARIS

Père Tanguy

OIL ON CANVAS, 25 x 19″

COLLECTION STAVROS NIARCHOS

AMONG THE PEOPLE van Gogh knew in the art world of Paris, Père Tanguy was closest to his image of simple humanity. This warm, friendly man, devoted to the struggling or unrecognized artists who came to his shop, was a Breton of radical convictions; he had taken part in the Commune of 1871, had been exiled and amnestied, and now sold artists' supplies in a little store which was a center for the Impressionists and the younger *avant-garde*; there one could see Pissarro, Cézanne, and Gauguin, and also their paintings. Van Gogh made at least three portraits of Tanguy. This one is remarkable for the combination of a naïvely realistic view—the centered, perfectly frontal figure, which reminds us both of medieval art and the primitives of photography—with a complex setting of works of art, mainly Japanese. The idea of the portrait figure among objects of art was common then among artists with a high culture and curiosity; examples are Manet's portrait of Zola and Degas' of the painter Tissot.

With a self-consciousness rare in his portraits, van Gogh paints both his friendship and his love of an exotic art. The surroundings and the figure clash —a gay outdoor coloring in the first, more earnest tones in the second, dark blues and browns of a scale closer to the humanity of the sitter. Yet the whole is a joyous harmony of bright and deep colors. Bold touches of green and red in the face and hands unite the figure to the surroundings; a surprising vermilion line traced freely along the costume repeats the red lines of the background. The diagonal arms, legs, and lapels are symmetrical counterparts of unmarked diagonals implicit in the pairing of similar elements in the Japanese works. Tanguy's homely features and, above all, the eyes, are powerfully done, with a loving search of the qualities of the friend. The face is intensely alive; the man's spirit radiates from a hidden region between the eyes, determining the radiation of the other features and the brush strokes. An equal life and firmness are transmitted to the tightly joined hands.

The Japanese heads are painted in pale flat tones, faithful to the originals and in polar contrast to Tanguy's face—a clear sign that van Gogh understood an essential difference between Far Eastern and European art, for which man had a deeper meaning.

PAINTED MARCH 1888, ARLES

The Pink Orchard

OIL ON CANVAS, 25¾ x 31¾"

STEDELIJK MUSEUM, AMSTERDAM *(V. W. van Gogh Collection)*

THE ORCHARD IN BLOSSOM, van Gogh's first welcoming encounter in the South, to which he had come in expectation of a healing, revitalizing nature, was for him an intoxicating vision, and it is this ecstasy that, pervading his work, sets it apart from the familiar Impressionist joy in light and atmospheric color. The trees raise to the sky a broad mass of immaterial whiteness and pinkness—more a floating emanation than a mass—scattered and suspended in a sky of equally varied tones, and playing against the interspersed phantom leafage and nerve-thin branchings which in places acquire a visionary aspect that recalls both Far Eastern painting and the discreet beauty and tenderness of the distant elements in early Western landscapes. All this intricate upper region of the picture—blossoms, sky, and arboreal network—coalesces into an overpowering pungency and intoxication of sensation in which the observer must lose himself. Without apparent order, an explosion of fragrance radiates and expands, filling its space, like the long horizontal clouds, in vaguely suggested diagonal and vertical directions.

In contrast to the enchanting diffuseness of the upper zone, the lower half of the picture is more solid and stable, with large areas of green and reddish color and the sturdiness of the irregular tree trunks, whose recurrent blue verticals repeat in color and oppose in direction the blue bandings of the sky. But here too is a palpitation of feeling realized in the streaking of color, the reds and the yellows—a streaking which in its deliberate verticality provides a contrast to the upper zone, and yet retains something of the latter's freedom and revery through the shapeless or unstressed patterning of the areas which they form. Uncommitted to the technique of a school, van Gogh's brushwork ranges from these neatly aligned strokes of red to the thick formless patches that convey in a magical undefinable manner the quality of blossoms in the air.

14

PAINTED MAY 1888

The Drawbridge

OIL ON CANVAS, 20¼ x 26⅜"

WALLRAF-RICHARTZ MUSEUM, COLOGNE

A DELICATE POETIC VISION that suggests the art of the Far East: dominant sky and water, few objects, little tension and crossing of forms, an approach to a peaceful revery. A distant cloud is most solid and tangibly painted. Aligned in a horizontal band along the horizon is a file of varied objects of an immaterial quality, each one delightful to the eye: houses, blue as the sky, slender cypresses of delicate stroke, an enchanting miniature horse and carriage and rider, the drawbridge slender and filmy like a spider's web, and, at the extreme right, light blue houses with red-striped rooftops permeated by the light. What a surprise is the inner bluish wall of the stone bridge, transparent like the water below, itself the bridge between the water and the sky!

16

PAINTED JUNE 1888, ARLES

Fishing Boats on the Beach at Saintes-Maries

OIL ON CANVAS, 25⅜ x 31⅞″

STEDELIJK MUSEUM, AMSTERDAM *(V. W. van Gogh Collection)*

VAN GOGH HAS DESCRIBED WITH JOY his visit to the Mediterranean shore near Arles at the fishing village of Saintes-Maries, where he painted and drew for several days. It was a new world for him, and he responded to it with his usual eagerness and excitement.

In the picture of the fishing boats, two different kinds of vision are united in one work: nature seen as light and airy, in countless tones of high-keyed color, ever changing and vibrant through universal contrast; on the other hand, man's objects, the boats, drawn precisely and painted in flat airless tones of primary color. The pearly softness of the seascape becomes a setting for the hard, firmly compartmented colors of the boats. But these boats, disposed along the beach beside one another, overlapping and with crossing masts, make an intricate network of spots and colored lines, which participate in the unstable airy shiftings of the natural tones, in the irregular patterns of the seashore and waves and the vast currents of the shapeless clouds, This network of the boats is a typical pattern of van Gogh's vision; it had appeared already in his Dutch period in the drawings of trees, and as in those early works, the branchings of the boat are drawn with unflagging devotion to the detailed individual shapes.

As the color ranges from the frank primary hues of the boats to tones of iridescence in the sky, with delicate blues, greens and lavenders, and nameless sandy tones, blendings of cool, neutralized yellow, tan, and brown—Impressionist in the subtle discriminations and pairings of cool and warm—so in the application of the paint there is a corresponding span from thin, flecked, and transparent touches, to thick and mat.

18

PAINTED JULY 1888, ARLES

La Mousmé

OIL ON CANVAS, 28⅞ x 23¾"

NATIONAL GALLERY OF ART, WASHINGTON, D. C.
(Chester Dale Collection, Loan)

A MOST SYMPATHETIC PORTRAIT in which van Gogh has tried to combine the
subtlest painting of nuanced tones in atmosphere and light with his new joyous sentiment of pure color and large, strong contrasts. The first quality we
see in the delicate modeling of the face, with little touches of warm and cool
tones, with almost imperceptible differences, as in the painting of the upper
lip against the surrounding skin, the whole suggesting by its soft transitions
and pallor a corresponding feminine quality. The light background toned
with a delicately emergent greenness belongs to the same family of color.
Against these rare phantom tones sing the intense, abundant stripes and spots
of orange, blue, and red, in the costume of the girl. Beautiful are the temper-
ing, more neutral colors of the arches of the chair—the dark pole of the background color. The chair together with the hands break up the immensity of the
spotted skirt into striking areas whose rhythm continues into the light-green
area in the lower right—a subdivision in sharpest contrast to the simplicity of
the upper body, yet tied to the latter through the curved and alternating stripes
of the bodice. The silhouette, as always with van Gogh, is vigorous and in-
terestingly contrived. Many fine little touches of color show his alertness as a
composer: the bit of blue on the collar, the dark violet and greenish tones in
the hair, the blue strokes in the left eye and between the lips, the ochres in
the ear and the jaw, the long curved file of modeled orange buttons which rise
from the ornamental, flat orange spots below, and, isolated against the cool
greenish background, the dainty, bizarre ends of red ribbon.

Of the subject van Gogh wrote to his brother: "If you know what a
'mousmé' is (you will know when you have read Loti's *Madame Chrysan-
thème*), I have just painted one. . . . A 'mousmé' is a Japanese girl—Provençal
in this case—12 to 14 years old. . . ."

20

Old Peasant (Patience Escalier)

OIL ON CANVAS, 27¾ x 22¾"

PRIVATE COLLECTION, LONDON

COMING TO PROVENCE FROM PARIS, van Gogh rediscovered the peasantry which had been his chief subject during his first years as a painter in Holland. This Mediterranean peasant is formed of the sun as well as the earth; his substance glows, without losing its earthy brownness; his blue cape and the burnt orange background are an inversion of the Provençal sky and earth. Most compelling, however, is the profound image of the man which, speaking to us at first through the eyes and then through the whole face, also conveys his strength through the masterfully drawn hands, and finally through the posture, the costume, the very partitioning of the space which he dominates. Of a rugged force, of a great simplicity and frankness in its large aspect, the portrait is focused upon a face of unsoundable depth and complication. Every feature is a world with its own shapes, colors, movement, and character, all the features uniting in the gravity of this ancient peasant nature fixed in earnest attention. The sheer power of representation is astounding: the luminosity of the red-fringed eyes, the colorful shagginess of the beard, all infused with the robustness and vitality of the varied brushwork that seems to follow pre-ordained paths and evokes an organic rhythm of the head. Great taste— let us say more rightly great understanding — appears in the gradation and contrast of the parts with respect to fullness of detail: the supreme region of the face, which contains all the colors of the painting like the palette source, under the brown shading brim, uniform in color; the yellow hat above, simple though more broken; the blue smock, complementary to the background in color, still more divided, and related in its many folds to the streaking of the beard; the three red spots of the cravat and the sleeves in a strong, concentrated pattern enclosing the hands, and supporting the head. This is perhaps the last realistic portrait of a peasant in the tradition of Western painting. It is perhaps also the only great portrait of a peasant.

PAINTED AUGUST 1888, ARLES

Oleanders

OIL ON CANVAS, 23⅝ x 28¾″

COLLECTION CHARLES SUYDAM CUTTING, NEW YORK

IN PLACING A COPY of Emile Zola's *La Joie de Vivre (The Joy of Living)* beside the jug of blooming oleanders, van Gogh announces to us the sense of his love of flowers. They rise and spread across the breadth of the picture like the blossoming trees of his spring landscapes. Heavy, profuse, fertile, these fragrant flowers are painted with a virile touch in circling strokes and thick parallel dabs, in sharpest contrast to the spiky, entangled green leaves outlined in black—the carriers of another vitality. Opposing and completing this span of reds and greens are the yellow and violet chords of the books, the table shadow, and the jug; between these pairs of complementaries mediates the yellow-green background, a strong note in harmony with both. This is not, however, a system of parceled decorative coloring: in the rich variation, interweaving, and stepping of tones, it retains the vibrancy and freedom of van Gogh's landscapes. Pink tones in the flowers approach the color of the table, and their whites, the edge of the book. The purple handle makes a triad with the flowers and the lilac shadow. The yellow band at the neck of the jug reappears as wavy stripes in the bouquet. The green of the leaves reappears in a cooler whitened tone at the base of the jug, and in brusque strokes at the right of the table, but also in the ornament of the jug; and this turquoise note returns unexpectedly among the leaves themselves. The strongest accents of red in the flowers are applied again with great daring along the edge of the table—a pure artistic decision, unmotivated by nature. The lilac shadow is another bold choice, justified by its place between the yellow book, the turquoise and blue-violet vase, and the yellow-green of the background. Striking to modern eyes is the drawing of the two books; odd in perspective, they form a succession of oblong and triangular strips, distinct in texture, which we find again in late Cubist designs. Magnificent in audacity beside the carefully drawn leaves is the painting of the table, joyous in its abandon and in the variety of colors and brush strokes. Like most of van Gogh's still lifes, this one possesses a high luminosity together with an astonishing firmness and tangibility of the objects.

PAINTED AUGUST 1888, ARLES

Sunflowers

OIL ON CANVAS, 36⅜ x 28⅞"

TATE GALLERY, LONDON

FOR THE DECORATION OF HIS ROOM, Vincent conceived a series of panels of sun-
flowers against backgrounds of yellow and blue. He had already painted these
golden flowers in Paris, lying separately on the table. His new conception was
more lyrical, an effort to possess the full radiance of these joy-giving flowers.
His enthusiasm for them announces the aesthetic of the 1890s, which drew
from the advanced biological and moral ideas of the time a kind of aesthetic
vitalism, a confidence in nature as a model of health and fulfillment through
growth and latent instinctive energies of the individual.

It is therefore not the traditional decorative still life of varied flowers but a
piece of the sun, a poem of joy in light and intense growth. Vincent had to rise
with the sun and paint these plants rapidly in early morning before they faded.
The yellow sunlight colors the entire canvas; it is indeed a composition in yellow. With little formality or searching, van Gogh has found an arrangement
which is free, balanced, and generous in substance, exhibiting the whole scale
of the qualities of this giant flower. His brush, with its usual directness, seeks
out the varied textures and tones of petals, disks, leaves, and stems against
the common luminous ground.

PAINTED SEPTEMBER 1888, ARLES

The Night Café

OIL ON CANVAS, 27½ x 35″

YALE UNIVERSITY ART GALLERY, NEW HAVEN
(Bequest of Stephen Carlton Clark, 1961)

VAN GOGH JUDGED THIS PICTURE which he painted for his landlord to pay the rent, "one of the ugliest I have done." Yet it gave him great joy to paint, and there are few works on which he has written with more conviction.

He has gone here beyond the agreeable side of the café world, imaged by the Impressionists, to its darker disquieting moments. The homeliness of the drawing, the interest in objects, the pervading moral concern, remind us of his Holland works. And indeed he spoke of it as "the equivalent though different, of the *Potato Eaters*," which it recalls by its lamplight; it is a powerful corresponding image of an opposite human condition—of the dissipated and homeless. But let us quote his own strong description.

"I have tried to express the terrible passions of humanity by means of red and green.

"The room is blood red and dark yellow with a green billiard table in the middle; there are four lemon-yellow lamps with a glow of orange and green. Everywhere there is a clash and contrast of the most alien reds and greens in the figures of little sleeping hooligans, in the empty dreary room, in violet and blue. The blood red and yellow green of the billiard table contrast with the soft tender Louis XV green of the counter on which there is a nosegay in rose color. The white coat of the patron, on vigil in a corner of this furnace, turns lemon yellow, or pale luminous green."

Some days later, he wrote: "I have tried to express the idea that the café is a place where one can ruin one's self, run mad or commit a crime. So I have tried to express as it were the powers of darkness in a low drink shop . . . and all this in an atmosphere like a devil's furnace, of pale sulphur."

In his account, van Gogh says nothing of one of the most powerful effects: the absorbing perspective that draws us headlong past empty chairs and tables into hidden depths behind a distant doorway—an opening like the silhouette of the standing figure. To the impulsive rush of these converging lines he opposes the broad horizontal band of red, full of scattered objects: the lights with their great haloes of concentric touches, the green clock at the midnight hour, and the bouquet of flowers, painted with an incredible fury of thick patches against the smooth wall above the crowd of bottles.

28

PAINTED OCTOBER 1888, ARLES

The Sower

OIL ON CANVAS, 13 x 16⅛″

STEDELIJK MUSEUM, AMSTERDAM *(V. W. van Gogh Collection)*

IN THIS TINY CANVAS, van Gogh wished to apply the lessons he had learned from Japanese art: composition of strong diagonals, objects cut by the frame, flat areas of pure color, whimsical shapes determined by the irregularities of nature. He retains, however, the full evidence of the brush and the impetus of the hand, which is foreign to the Japanese prints he loved; and a nuancing of atmospheric colors in light and shadow that is strictly Western. Not pure intense colors, but rare tones like the apple-green sky which take the observer out of the familiar world and awaken him to astonishment and revery and submerged currents of feeling. In van Gogh's conception of the figure and the tree, there is a mysterious affinity in color, silhouette, and direction, like an unexpected rhyme which unites otherwise unconnected words and gives a greater resonance to both.

Decisive for the mood of the work is the vision of the distant colorful world through the dark neutralized tones of the foreground objects, and the position of the gigantic sun between them.

In the network of lines, we may observe van Gogh's great intuitive command of the harmony of directions and his freedom in deploying the elements given by nature.

Vincent's Chair

OIL ON CANVAS, 36⅛ x 28¾"

TATE GALLERY, LONDON

THIS SURPRISING THEME is one of a pair. Together with it, van Gogh painted Gauguin's chair on which he set a lighted candle and two books. A fascinating diptych that is more than a still life, for it evokes and symbolizes the human beings to whom these objects belonged, like the attributes of saints in old pictures. When his father died, van Gogh had painted a still life with the old man's pipe and pouch.

The chair, a familiar object that we scarcely know after years of use, has been transposed to the canvas with great fervor; its form and weight and rigidity and texture have been realized in a most complete manner. Van Gogh's conviction about the importance of this chair penetrates us and holds us, until we feel a mystery in its presence. This mystery grows when we see the chair in its surroundings which are also tangible objects, but incomplete; none is an object-for-a-spectator, none has been singled out for a privileged presentation. Underneath the simplicity of the objects, we encounter the difficult involvements of coexistence in the unsteady, bewildering crisscross of the chair legs and rungs with the joints of the tiles—an involvement that is mostly an affair of chance juxtaposition and perspective, the observer's odd way of looking, which determines an intricacy useless for our knowledge of the chair and ordinarily unnoticed. But not altogether so, for the oblique position of the chair frees it from the surroundings and suggests the freedom of the human being in this rigid geometrical world.

Within the conflicting, intersecting systems of the lines, van Gogh has introduced connecting parallels and continuities. Clearest is the yellowish right angle traced on the door and fitted precisely to the leg of the chair. At the foremost lower rung a zigzag line of the floor reaches from leg to leg. The crossing lines of the rush seat belong as much to the network of the floor as of the chair.

The color too has an aspect of intricacy in the scale and contact of tones. In the high-keyed scheme, the richly varied yellow, strengthened by the white wall, lies between the orange-red tiles and the cool green door; and is recalled in both through yellowish lines which repeat the directions of the chair. Correspondingly, the blue-green of the door reappears in blue outlines of the yellow rungs and legs, and the darkest brown tones of the tiles in other contours of the chair.

PAINTED OCTOBER 1889, SAINT-REMY

Landscape with Olive Trees

OIL ON CANVAS, 28½ x 35½"

COLLECTION THE HON. AND MRS. JOHN HAY WHITNEY, NEW YORK

VAN GOGH'S PASSIONATENESS fills the entire landscape—ground, trees, mountains, clouds—with a tumultuous heaving motion. It is more powerful and imaginative than anything in later Expressionist art, which proceeded from a similar, emotionally charged vision of nature. It is also more attached to the real, for in the common movement that seems to issue from an underlying force, overwhelming all objects, these retain their individuality, their unique rhythms. It is the decided character of each horizontal zone of this turbulent work that keeps the picture from succumbing to the dullness of chaos, which so often results from an artist's immersion in pure feeling. The visionary cloud, with blue and yellow streaks and wavy outline, vaguely organic (one can see in it a wraith-like mother and child), the fantastic rugged silhouette of the mountain with the perforated rocky mass, like a ruined castle,—these are new forms of great power. The color too shows an ordered variation, striking in its freshness: the light cloud against the cold greenish-blue sky; below, the warmer, light greens of the olive trees against the dark blue of the mountains; and in the lower half of the work the churning sea of the earth with coiling bands of light and shadow, of yellow, blue, and green. Characteristic of the drawing, besides the extraordinary length of the wavy lines— van Gogh compared the lines with those of old woodcuts—is the depth of their hollows. At first view overpowering in its sustained movement, the landscape offers to continued meditation a surprising range of qualities: the soft floating cloud and the hard rocks; the bland uniformity of the sky color and the fierce changing contrasts of the space below; the furious storm of the brush strokes in the trees and the rhythmical waviness and clarity of the mountains; the uniform local color of sky, mountains and trees and the wild mottling of the earth. In all these, a pervading luminosity, from the distant cloud to the earth beneath the olive trees.

PAINTED MAY 1890, SAINT-REMY

Road with Cypresses

OIL ON CANVAS, 35¾ x 28″

KROLLER-MULLER STATE MUSEUM, OTTERLO, HOLLAND

BY FORCE OF VAN GOGH'S ECSTATIC EXALTATION, a real landscape acquires an
unearthly character. The central place of the dominating cypress, between
the sun and moon with their vast haloes, intimates a fervent communion of
the artist with his vision. The cypress, which he had admired for its geometrical purity of shape and likened to an obelisk, is a shaggy straining form,
a vertical forest formed of two trees indistinguishably merged, a tormented
living spire ascending with abrupt shifts from side to side out of the picture,
above the sun and moon. The earth is invested with similar writhing shapes,
in the yellow field and the cascading stream of the road; there are minor
echoes in the green patches which also resemble the quivering trees in the
far distance. A strange contrast to all this grandiose agitation are the figures
on the road, the horse and yellow cart and the distant lighted house. Poetic
elements of a touching, homely realism in the evening scene, they have also
their precise places in the movement of the visionary whole. But so powerful
is the contrast of the central vertical cypress and the unstable diagonals of
the earth that the picture wavers between these opposite pulls. The artist
strains to unite them; moon, sun and evening star lie on a strong diagonal
slightly bent like the edge of the road below, and a great cloud inclines to the
earth from the star. The impassioned execution, the common tempo of strokes
throughout the work, help to fuse the antagonistic parts. In a world of sharply
opposed and crossing objects with pointed forms there is a compelling con-
tinuity in the varied paths of the brush strokes—concentric in the sky, parallel,
wavy, and convergent on the earth, flame-like in the trees. Through its cool
color the sky, ranging from deep blue to white in gradual transitions, belongs
with the lighter road below. The dark green cypresses, of another span, are
tied to both the yellow field and the blue sky; and the yellows and orange
tones of the sun and moon, the yellows of the carriage, the red of the dwarfed
cypress trunks, connect their widely separated zones by couplings of color
along tilted and crossed axes. Throughout, a masterful precision in the small
touches of color, especially beautiful in the movement and nuancing of the
indescribable color of the road.

PAINTED SEPTEMBER 1889, SAINT-REMY

Portrait of the Artist

OIL ON CANVAS, 22⅜ x 17⅛"

COLLECTION THE HON. AND MRS. JOHN HAY WHITNEY, NEW YORK

THE PERVADING BLUE, WARMER, MORE VIOLET, in the background, cooler in the clothes, shapes a mood that we cannot name but of which the inward-pointing nature is clear. Not only is the blueness shared by the costume and the "abstract" surroundings, but the live brushwork forming this environment follows in its interwoven traces the changing edges of the head like a halo around it; at the same time it conforms in its vehement flow to the impassioned rhythms of the strokes that model the costume and the hair. Out of a dark hollow in the center of this blue emerges the head with a glowing intensity. The face is mostly in shadow, a beautifully painted transparent shadow, rich in greens and blues, a dark film through which peer the red-rimmed eyes, probing and sad. Painting the hair, the moustache and beard, van Gogh forgets the shadow, giving to these parts their full intensity as exceptional luminous colors with interspersed greens, madders, and reds. A light shadow stream, bridged by a knot, rises from the upward-thrust, obtuse edge of the palette which echoes the face. Here the colors of the painting are laid out in a horizontal line, a surprising adaptation to the edge of the canvas, in defiance of the perspective of the palette itself. The brushes emerge from it like the lines of the smock, forming a fanwise succession from the violet patch below to the wedge of background above—triangular shapes repeated and inverted in the areas beyond, and culminating in the pathetic region of the right eye. The head turned to its right, together with the palette, gives to that side a more abrupt, constricted, tense quality; the other half is rounded and continuous in its forms. At the same time van Gogh, with an approach to classic sensibility in his new curvilinear style, has continued the hollow edge of the face in the line of the right shoulder, producing by this large crescent form a hidden symmetry of the two sides of the head and shoulders in a three-quarters pose.

This portrait in its jewelled perfection and depth of feeling permits us to measure van Gogh's great advance since his Paris portraits; it corresponds to a deeper self-insight as well as to an enormous growth in power of expression.

ON PAGE 7:

PAINTED SEPTEMBER 1888, ARLES

Sidewalk Café at Night

OIL ON CANVAS, 31 x 24¾″

KROLLER-MULLER STATE MUSEUM, OTTERLO, HOLLAND

THIS PICTURESQUE WORK recalls van Gogh's mood when he wrote that "the night is more alive and more richly colored than the day." The color is profuse and the eye wanders along the stepped or dovetailed edges of neighboring areas— irregular fragmented shapes fitted to each other like a jigsaw puzzle design. For the roving, unengaged vision the upward dimension is no less important and expressive than the depth. The silhouette of the starry sky is the key to the patterning of the whole; the poetic idea of the work—the double illu- mination and contrast of the café and the night sky—is developed through this jagged form. Delightful and spectacular as it is, the painting is less deeply absorbing, less concentrated than the best of van Gogh.